short

long

hard

soft

The **First Skills** series includes seven books designed to help parents amuse, interest and at the same time teach their children. **Colours and shapes** and **abc** contribute to the child's early understanding of the reading process. **Counting** teaches him to recognize and understand simple numbers. **Telling the time** helps him to relate the time on a clock face to his everyday life and activities. **Big and little** deals with words that describe relative sizes and positions, all shown through objects and scenes that will be familiar to the young child. **Everyday words** helps him to enjoy and practise his vocabulary. **Verbs** will develop his early reading and language skills. In each book, bright, detailed, interesting illustrations combine with a simple and straightforward text to present fundamental concepts clearly and comprehensibly.

Talk about the relative sizes and shapes of familiar objects: 'look at this big bus! It's much bigger than our car, isn't it? But your bike is even smaller, isn't it!' Talk about your family. Who is the tallest? Who has the loudest voice? Games can be about relative size, too. Children will enjoy stretching their arms up and out to become as big as they can, and then curling up into a little ball to become very small.

A catalogue record for this book is available form the British Library

Published by Ladybird Books Ltd
80 Strand London WC2R 0RL
A Penguin Company

2 4 6 8 10 9 7 5 3
© LADYBIRD BOOKS LTD MMVI

LADYBIRD and the device of a Ladybird are trademarks of Ladybird Books Ltd

Printed in Italy

big and little

by Lesley Clark
photography by Garie Hind

These socks are the same.

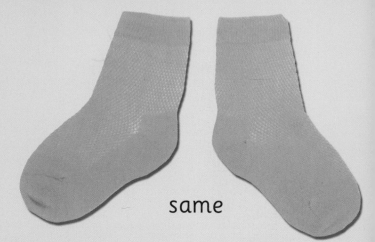

same

But these socks are different.

different

Are these slippers the same?

Are these slippers the same or different?

Use practical everyday situations, such as tidying up, dressing and playing, to help your child explore things that are the same and things that are different.

Teddy bears, teddy bears – just the same!

same

different

The elephant is big, but the mouse is little.

big

little

Look at your toys.

Are they all different sizes?

Talk to your child about his own toys. Can he find one that is big? Can he find one that is little?

The bear with the blue and yellow bowl is large. The bear with the yellow bowl is middle-sized.

large

middle-sized

The bear with the green bowl
is small.

small

These things are cold...

cold

and these are hot.

hot

NEVER touch or go near hot
things on your own.

Talking about these pictures of hot things will
help your child to understand that they are
dangerous and can hurt.

Jenny and her doll have their eyes open. They are awake.

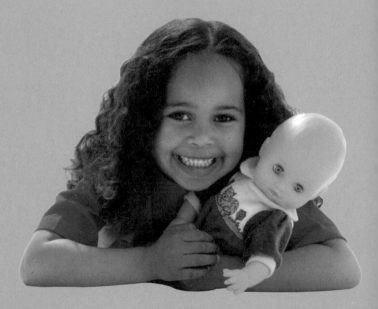

awake

Jenny and her doll have their eyes shut. They are asleep.

asleep

This glass is empty.

empty

Fill it up with juice – now it is full!

full

Sally's bucket is heavy!

heavy

Now her bucket
is light!

light

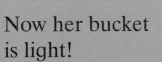

Play water games at bath times, filling and emptying lots of different sized containers.

Look at the children, all in a row –
one, two, three, four.

Who is the tallest?

Who is the shortest?

shortest

tallest

Children love being measured. Keep a height chart in your child's bedroom as a visual reminder of how much he has grown.

Humpty is fat,
but the soldier is thin.

fat   thin

The beanbag is soft to sit on.

soft

The rock is hard.

hard

Where would you rather sit?

One scarf is short.

The other is long.

short   long

Emma's hair is short, but Laura's hair is long.

short   long

Is your hair short or long?

Look for other long and short things in the photograph. Emma has short sleeves, short socks, etc. Laura has long versions of the same things.

Climb up to the top of the ladder...
one, two, three!

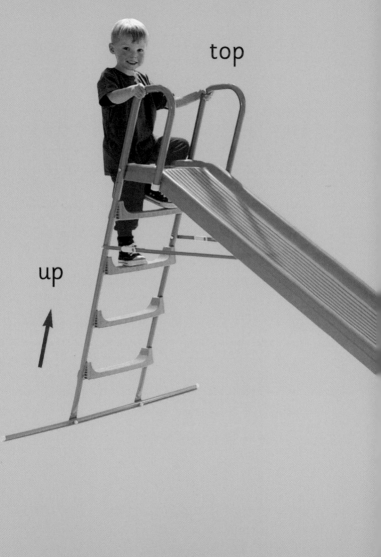

top

up

Whoosh...down to the bottom,
quick as can be!

down

bottom

Get on the bike...
one, two, three – go!

on

One, two, three – stop!
Now it is time to climb off.

off

Open the door and say...

Hello!

open

Close the door, now it is time to go.

Goodbye!

closed

Can you find the things that are the same?

teddy

teapot

slipper

sock